KV-648-566

WITHDRAWN FROM STOCK

WITHDRAWN FROM STOCK
532285

WITHDRAWN FROM STOCK

WITHDRAWN FROM STOCK

WITHDRAWN FROM STOCK

WITHDRAWN FROM STOCK

WITHDRAWN FROM STOCK

(433)

CREATING A
LEARNING
ORGANISATION

Better Management Skills

This highly popular range of inexpensive paperbacks covers all areas of basic management. Practical, easy to read and instantly accessible, these guides will help managers to improve their business or communication skills. Those marked * are available on audio cassette.

The books in this series can be tailored to specific company requirements. For further details, please contact the publisher, Kogan Page, telephone 0171 278 0433, fax 0171 837 6348.

Be a Successful Supervisor
Be Positive
Building High Performance Teams
Business Creativity
Business Etiquette
Coaching Your Employees
Conducting Effective Interviews
Counselling Your Staff
Creative Decision-making
Creative Thinking in Business
Delegating for Results
Develop Your Assertiveness
Effective Employee Participation
Effective Meeting Skills
Effective Performance Appraisals*
Effective Presentation Skills
Empowerment
First Time Supervisor
Get Organised!
Goals and Goal Setting
How to Communicate Effectively*
How to Develop a Positive Attitude*
How to Develop Assertiveness
How to Manage Organisational Change
How to Motivate People*
How to Plan Your Competitive Strategy
How to Understand Financial Statements
How to Write a Staff Manual
Improving Employee Performance
Improving Relations at Work
Leadership Skills for Women
Make Every Minute Count*
Making TQM Work
Managing Cultural Diversity at Work
Managing Disagreement Constructively
Managing Organisational Change
Managing Part-time Employees
Managing Quality Customer Service
Marketing for Success
Memory Skills in Business
Mentoring
Office Management
Personnel Testing
Process Improvement
Productive Planning
Project Management
Quality Customer Service
Rate Your Skills as a Manager
Sales Training Basics
Self-managing Teams
Successful Negotiation
Successful Presentation Skills
Successful Telephone Techniques
Systematic Problem-solving and Decision-making
Team Building
Training Methods that Work
The Woman Manager

CREATING A LEARNING ORGANISATION

Barbara J Braham

KOGAN
PAGE

Copyright © Crisp Publications Inc 1995

All rights reserved. No part of this book may be reproduced or transmitted in any form or by any means now known or to be invented, electronic or mechanical, including photocopying, recording, or by any information storage or retrieval system, without written permission from the author or publisher, except for the brief inclusion of quotations in a review.

First published in the United States of America in 1995 by Crisp Publications Inc, 1200 Hamilton Court, Menlo Park, California 94025, USA.

Reprinted 1998

This edition first published in Great Britain in 1996 by Kogan Page Ltd, 120 Pentonville Road, London N1 9JN.

British Library Cataloguing in Publication Data

A CIP record for this book is available from the British Library.

ISBN 0-7494-1995-4

Typeset by BookEns Ltd, Royston, Herts.
Printed in England by Clays Ltd, St Ives plc

Contents

CHAPTER 1
Why Become a Learning Organisation?

Learning is one of the few competitive advantages available today. This book gives you the tools to assess whether your organisation is a learning organisation. You'll discover how not to impede learning, and how to support the natural desire in each person to become a lifelong learner.

Learning organisation checklist

Complete the following checklist. Tick each statement that is true for your organisation to discover the current learning climate. Give an example of the statements you ticked in the space provided.

☐ **1.** Learning is integrated into everything people do.

_____

☐ **2.** Learning for learning's sake is encouraged and often rewarded.

_____

☐ **3.** Our organisation strongly supports teamwork, creativity, empowerment and quality.

_____

☐ **4.** Employees are trusted to choose the courses that they need.

_____

☐ **5.** People with different job titles from different departments learn together.

_____

☐ **6.** We promote mentoring relationships to enhance learning.

_____

☐ **7.** Learning is integrated into meetings, work groups and work processes.

_____

☐ **8.** All individuals, regardless of position, have equal access to learning.

_____

☐ **9.** We treat mistakes as learning opportunities.

_____

☐ **10.** We have initiated cross-training and reward employees who learn a wider range of job skills.

_____

It is hoped that you were able to tick each box, as all ten items are found in true learning organisations. However, if you have items without ticks congratulations; you have just learned that your organisation has areas that need development. And that is what this book is all about!

What is a learning organisation?

A learning organisation is an organisation that prioritises learning.

Learning is simultaneously both a process and a value. Ideally, every individual in the company, regardless of position or length of service, is committed to being better tomorrow than they are today – through learning. The organisation as a whole is committed to continual improvement of every facet of itself, its products and its services – by learning about learning. As both the individual and the organisation develop, employees will feel a renewed connection to their work, customers will be better served and the organisation will create a future for itself.

A learning organisation is set apart from other organisations in these ways:

- Learning is integrated into everything people do; it's a regular part of the job, not 'something extra' you add on.
- Learning is a process, not an event.
- Cooperation is the foundation of all relationships.
- Individuals themselves evolve and grow, and in the process transform the organisation.
- The learning organisation is creative; individuals re-create the organisation.
- The organisation learns from itself; employees teach the organisation about efficiency, quality improvement and innovation.
- It is enjoyable and exciting to be part of a learning organisation.

In the learning organisation, motivation is recognised as being inherent in each person. With a shared vision and commitment to that vision, people will motivate themselves to learn. Rather than being threatened to learn, it's assumed that individuals and teams will proactively set their own learning agendas. Initially, the organisation may need to provide resources and coaching to help people learn how to do this.

There are two significant differences between the content of learning inside a learning organisation and in other organisations.

1. Employees in a learning organisation learn about the business side of their company. They have access to more information than ever before on sales targets, marketing plans and financial statements. In a learning organisation, this information is no longer for management or executive eyes only. With employees empowered to make more decisions, they need to understand those decisions in the overall context of the business.

2. Individuals learn how to use themselves as tools. Never before has this been so important. The learning organisation has discovered that 'soft is hard'. In other words, interpersonal skills, creativity, responsiveness to change and learning how to learn are the skills that serve a person and therefore the organisation in the global marketplace of today. The learning organisation needs individuals capable of managing themselves; people who understand that the skill with which they manage themselves will determine how others respond to them. Technical skill alone will not guarantee success.

Communication in the learning organisation has taken a quantum leap. Today the purpose of communication goes beyond speaking clearly; communication is now attempting to create community. In such an environment, honesty, self-awareness, cooperation and acceptance are the staples. Communication of such depth facilitates learning, about oneself and about the work. For perhaps the first time, it is not necessary to erect a barrier between who you are on the job and who you are at home.

- You can bring your whole self to work.
- You are enriched.
- Your work is enriched.
- Everyone learns.

The organisation's new direction

The learning organisation perceives itself as a living system. Every part is connected to every other part. As in a living organism, there is enormous pressure to maintain homeostasis: If you try to change one part, other parts of the system will make a concerted effort to restore the status quo. Once change has in fact occurred, however, it will affect the entire system. *Systems thinking* allows the organisation to focus on *systems change*, rather than searching for one guilty party when there's a problem.

What does a learning organisation learn? Everything. However, most organisations begin by focusing on one of these areas:

- Work products
- Work processes
- Teamwork
- Customers
- Systems thinking
- Mental models.

Quiz
True or false

Your organisation may already be well on its way towards becoming a learning organisation, or this may be your first introduction to the concept. Take the following true/false quiz to get a better understanding of how your organisation responds to the learning needs of employees.

	True	False
We work to remove barriers to learning.	☐	☐
We cultivate a learner friendly environment.	☐	☐
We identify tools our organisation can use to become a learning organisation.	☐	☐
We understand how adults learn and use that knowledge to our advantage.	☐	☐
We use various tools to assess employees' learning progress.	☐	☐

	True	False
We acknowledge that people learn from experience.	☐	☐
We recognise what type of learning is most appropriate for our situation.	☐	☐
We encourage each employee to become a lifelong learner.	☐	☐
We encourage employees to keep an open mind to learning.	☐	☐
We understand the factors that inhibit learning.	☐	☐
We know how to motivate people to learn.	☐	☐

Any statement marked false represents an area that needs to be developed as you create a learning organisation.

Why is learning so important?

Things are changing so fast today that it is difficult to keep up with the pace. People who can't keep up with changes may find themselves 'downsized' or 'rightsized' – or some other euphemism for *out of work*. A business that can't change in tune with the global marketplace probably has no future.

What's the answer? The answer is *learning*
It is one of the few, if not the only competitive advantage available today. Moreover, it is the healthiest response in a world of rapid change. The question is no longer *if* you will use available technology, from voice mail to computers, of *if* you will use the business techniques of problem solving, meeting facilitation and teamwork. The question today is how quickly, how efficiently, and how effectively can the people in your organisation become proficient in using the technologies.

Organisations and individuals who are able to learn with the greatest ease and speed will be the most successful in the future. Today a person cannot expect the current level of knowledge and expertise to serve him or her for years ahead. That assumption will result in unemployment and disillusionment. With knowledge and technology advancing so quickly, you don't have years to 'get up to speed'. The secret, then, is identifying the need to learn, and then setting yourself to the task quickly and efficiently.

Learning is not the same thing as acquiring knowledge any more than data is the same as information. When you learn, your behaviour changes. As Peter Senge wrote in *The Fifth Discipline*:*

> Real learning gets to the heart of what it means to be human. Through learning we re-create ourselves. Through learning we become able to do something we never were able to do. Through learning we reperceive the world and our relationship to it. Through learning we extend our capacity to create, to be part of the generative process of life. There is within each of us a deep hunger for this type of learning.

Senge is right – there is a deep hunger for learning. It is painful for individuals to stand by and watch their company inhibit learning. It is frustrating when employees can't apply what they know. It is discouraging when the organisation makes unnecessary mistakes. Standing by and watching this happen will damage people's spirits. Creating a learning organisation can restore that spirit to 'respirit' the workplace.

Exercise
Why your organisation might want to be a learning organisation
Tick all the reasons why your organisation might want to pursue becoming a learning organisation. Add your own reasons if they're not listed.

- ☐ To stay in business
- ☐ To remain competitive
- ☐ To be a leader in your field or industry

---

* Peter Senge, *The Fifth Discipline*, London: Business Books, 1993.

- ☐ Better to serve the needs of your customers/clients/patients
- ☐ To increase profitability
- ☐ To be a role model for your suppliers
- ☐ To prevent mistakes
- ☐ To avoid repeating mistakes
- ☐ To benefit from all the gifts your employees have to contribute
- ☐ To raise the organisation's collective IQ
- ☐ To create a motivating work environment
- ☐ To attract and retain outstanding employees
- ☐ To build on the organisation's strengths and previous successes
- ☐ To support the growth and development of your employees
- ☐ To 'respirit' the workplace
- ☐ To contribute new products/knowledge/services to the world
- ☐ To become better at what you do
- ☐ To implement your Total Quality Management programme
- ☐ To sustain your Total Quality Management programme
- ☐ To help employees learn how to work together more effectively
- ☐ _____
- ☐ _____

What investment is required?

Having anything of value requires an initial investment from you. If you want good health, you need to exercise, eat sensibly, maintain a positive attitude and get adequate rest.

What it will take
Time
If you want employees to commit themselves to learning, learning needs to be part of the regular working day – not an

add-on or an afterthought. Don't expect employees to prove their commitment to learning by doing it in their own time. Certainly they may give their own time, but if you want yours to be a learning organisation, then your commitment is to allocate time for learning. How much time is enough? It will vary depending on your industry and each person's specific role. In general, though, think about allocating 10 per cent of the working week. Yes, that's four hours every week dedicated to learning. You'll find that you'll recoup that time, however, in the elimination of wasted effort, duplication and bureaucratic confusion.

Money
Expect to spend money on training, training materials, time away from the job while learning, and on hiring internal and external experts. What percentage of your organisation's payroll is allocated to training? The industry average is 1.2 per cent. A minimum recommended standard is 2 per cent and 4 per cent if you're serious about becoming a learning organisation. Motorola invested 1.5 per cent in 1985; it saw such a return on its investment that by 1994 its commitment was up to 4 per cent.*

Communication
Employees need to understand why learning is important. There will also be an intensified need to keep people informed so that learning is conveyed from one part of the company to another.

What it will do
Produce change
Not all the changes will be easy or enjoyable. You may discover habits in yourself or traditions in your organisation that need to be changed. It will often be unclear initially whether the changes are beneficial. With change may come

* Business Week, 28 March 1994, pp 158–163.

stress, and you can expect resistance to the changes. As individuals learn, however, they'll put pressure on the organisation to change.

Test your ability to find balance
It is challenging for an organisation to pursue learning simultaneously while getting its usual work done. Too much focus on the process of learning, and the business slips; too little focus on learning, and the business slips. The point of balance is often elusive. Clarity of purpose is essential.

What investments will be easiest for your organisation to make?

_____

_____

Which ones will be most difficult?

_____

_____

Who is responsible for learning?

Both the organisation and its individual members have responsibility for learning. But for each of them, the responsibilities are different.

The organisation is responsible for providing learning opportunities and a structure that supports learning. Equally important, it needs to remove barriers to learning – learn how to get out of the way!

Even the best-designed learning structure, however, cannot *make* someone learn. The individuals within the organisation will need to use the opportunities made available to them. It is the individual who is responsible for translating knowledge into learning on a day-to-day basis.

When your company supports learning, it makes it easier for individual employees to learn. But even if learning is not a priority within an organisation, that does not absolve the individuals of their learning responsibilities. Each day, each experience, can be a learning experiment.

Take a moment now to think through your personal responsibility for and commitment to learning.

Why is learning important to you?

_____

_____

In what ways are you committed to learning?

_____

_____

What is your perception of your organisation's commitment to learning?

_____

_____

Why do you believe learning is important to your company at this time?

_____

_____

CHAPTER 2

What it Takes to Become a Learning Organisation

Tools important to a learning organisation

As Peter Senge said in *The Fifth Discipline*, becoming a learning organisation is not about emulating a 'model'. Rather, you create the learning environment as you go, based on your organisation, its customers, problems, markets and individual personalities. Aspiring learning organisations share many common characteristics, but perhaps the most important is a willingness to continue learning. Remember that no matter how much you learn, there is always more to learn.

In this section we will identify some of the tools your organisation can use in its quest to become a learning organisation. Many of the tools used by a learning organisation are also used by the traditional, hierarchical organisation (from now on, we'll call this the *telling organisation*). The difference lies in why the tools are used, who uses them, and when and where they are used. Before we examine those tools, take a look at the following chart. It summarises the differences, in terms of learning characteristics, between learning in the telling organisation and the learning organisation.

What it Takes to Become a Learning Organisation

Learning characteristic	Telling organisation	Learning organisation
Who learns?	People who are: 'sent'; rewarded; or related groups (ie, managers or sales people)	Everyone: all employees; all departments and levels
Who teaches?	In-house trainers or outside experts	People closest to the work, trainers, some 'experts'
Who is responsible?	Training Department	Everyone
What learning tools do people use?	Courses, on-the-job training (OTJ), mentoring, formal training, learning plans	Courses, OTJ training, learning plans, mentors, benchmarks, teams, personal reflection, partnerships
When do people learn?	When required, first few months on job, as needed	All the time, for long term
What skills do they learn?	Technical	Technical, business, interpersonal, how to learn
Where do they learn?	Classes, on the job	Classes, meetings, doing the work, everywhere
Time	Today's needs	Future needs
Feeling	Soulless	Spirited

Many organisations are confused by the 'how' – the tools – of learning. They mistakenly think that if they offer courses and have a tuition reimbursement programme, that makes them a learning organisation. But the tools, as you can see from the chart, are not what separates a learning organisation from a telling organisation. The tools are like bricks; you can use them to build a cathedral or a prison.

The tools and their continuums

Now let's explore each of the learning tools and how they are used differently by a telling and a learning organisation. Each tool is set up on a *continuum*. At the far left end of the continuum are indications of how the tool is used in a telling organisation, symbolised by a pyramid ($\triangle$). The telling organisation is characterised by control, competitiveness, short-term quantitative results, reactiveness and functional units that operate in silos (isolated units). The telling organisation 'works hard'. In your company today, this may be how one or more of these tools are being used.

At the right end of the continuum are indications of how the tool is used by organisations consciously trying to become learning organisations, symbolised by a circle ($\bigcirc$). These organisations are characterised by:

- Teamwork
- Cooperation
- Creativity
- Empowerment
- Quality.

The learning organisation 'works smart'. You may recognise your organisation at this end of the continuum, or perhaps you are somewhere in the middle.

As you read through each tool's description, mark the point on the continuum where you would place your organisation today, with the date. You may place your company all the way to the left, the right, or somewhere in between. Remember, this is an assessment tool, not a judgement tool.

Return to these continuums every six months. Notice where your organisation makes changes, and move your organisation forwards or backwards accordingly. You may even discover that your company has moved beyond the right end of the continuum.

Continuum 1. Tuition reimbursement

Place an X on the line to mark where your organisation is today, and date it.

Telling	**Learning**
● Job-related classes only	● Employee chooses classes
● Company controls degree programmes	● Non job-related coursework OK
● No class work/Job connection	● Part of comprehensive learning plan

Many companies have a tuition-reimbursement programme. According to the programme, an employee can attend certain pre-approved courses that are directly related to the job or are part of the requirements for a degree related to the job. To be reimbursed, the employee may be required to earn a certain grade or commit to a specified number of years of service. Rarely is any application made of the classroom learning to actual on-the-job tasks.

Companies moving towards the right end of the continuum will reimburse tuition for classes that are job-related as well as classes that aren't. For example, your company might pay for a secretary to take accounting courses. Most important, the learning organisation consciously seeks to integrate the classroom experience with the job. Sometimes partners or teams go to classes together to increase the on-the-job application. Other times, the integration takes place through conversation, using questions such as these:

● What are you learning?
● How can you apply it in this work setting?
● What questions does it provoke about how your work is being done?
● Can you complete any class projects using a real-life job situation?

1. What is your company's current policy regarding tuition reimbursement?

   _____

   _____

   _____

2. How many times have you taken advantage of this?

   _____

   _____

   _____

3. How many people in your department use tuition reimbursement?

   _____

   _____

   _____

4. What is in place to guide course selection?

   _____

   _____

   _____

Continuum 2. Formal training

Place an X on the line to mark where your organisation is today.

Telling
- Dictated by organisation

- Mandatory
- Generic courses

- Delivered by training staff or hired experts
- Limited offerings
- Stop-gap approach
- Cut in hard times
- Formal teacher–student relationship
- Used to 'fix'

Learning
- Employees trusted to choose needed courses
- Encouraged
- Customised to industry company/position
- Taught by line staff and/or dedicated trainers
- Self-paced training
- Integrated to the work
- Expanded in hard times
- Each one teaches one – staff learn to teach one another
- Used to develop

In the telling organisation, learning is like ice, rigid and frozen. Although both the training department and individuals feel that they're 'chipping away' at learning, it still remains a solid block that sits in the training department most of the time. When the block is sent to a department, it gets put on a shelf where it silently watches, not participating. Or individuals may attend a training programme and return excited about implementing a new idea, only to be told, 'That's not the way we do things here'. When there's a problem, one of the first solutions is to 'throw training at it'. In this environment – with training on the left end of the continuum – the risk is that while some individuals may learn, the organisation does not.

Contrast this with the learning organisation, where learning flows like a river through every department and location doing its work. As it moves from one department to another, it is enriched and carries along much more than it started with. Learning flourishes in the flowing river. The learning is integrated everywhere, and the organisation grows.

In the learning organisation, then, training is less an event and more of a process. Everyone gets involved, not just in learning, but also in teaching. People learn from one another, and the organisation learns from its employees, suppliers, vendors and customers. Instead of homogeneous training classes (managers with managers, secretaries with secretaries), learning groups have diversity in both job title and responsibility. In this environment, learning is not just a one-way street. Training is customised to meet the needs of specific groups and projects, rather than expecting the learners to adapt the training to their situation.

In telling organisations, training is an event that takes place when times are good. It is often for select groups of employees, perhaps salespeople or managers. It may even be perceived as either a perk or a punishment. You get the chance to go, or you're required to go. There isn't room for *wanting* to go. Consequently, when learning occurs, it is in isolated pockets around the organisation.

This changes in a learning organisation. No longer are learning events segregated into élite pockets of the company. Learning can happen any time, anywhere, with anyone. It becomes the responsibility of each person, not just the 'training department'. Knowledge flows both ways, and individuals continue to learn from the company while the company also learns from its employees.

Case study
Becoming a learning company

Pier 1, a 32-year-old importer of unique merchandise, is one example of a company whose training has moved from the left to the right end of the continuum. As other retailers began to carry merchandise similar to Pier 1's, it became increasingly difficult for Pier 1 to distinguish itself in the marketplace. After doing some customer surveys, the company decided to increase its selling and service expertise.

The first step was a training video-book programme on Quality Customer Service. Although a standard product, the programme was used as an 'event' to solve a problem, not as part of an integrated, graduated, usable programme.

Next, Pier 1 worked with an outside company to design a customised selling programme. This time the programme was attended and supported by all the executives before it was delivered to store managers across 25 regions by an interdisciplinary team. The programme signified a shift of focus from merchandise to selling and servicing. Once the managers had been trained, assistant managers were trained. These managers and assistant managers became the training force that introduced 10,000 associates to the new skills and the new focus. Thus the training programme has shifted from an event championed by the training department to a process integrated and 'owned' by everyone – from senior executives to individual associates

Most recently, the Pier 1 training department is compiling a video newsletter to support ongoing training. In many ways the newsletter looks similar to Pier 1's first video-book programme. The difference is that today learning is integrated into the company, and everyone owns the programme (not just the training department). Rather than mastery of a particular set of skills, the goal is continuous improvement of selling and servicing skills. Pier 1 continues to move towards the right end of the continuum.

Exercise
Your training options
Training comes in many packages. Tick the box by each one that your organisation uses.

- ☐ Internally developed programme
- ☐ 'Off the shelf.' In other words, the company purchases a prepared programme, often with leaders' guides to help your in-house trainers use it.
- ☐ Hire outside experts
- ☐ Public seminars
- ☐ Off-site executive programmes
- ☐ Customised books
- ☐ Customised videos

☐ Computer-based training
☐ Computer-aided instruction
☐ Off-the-shelf audio or video learning programmes.

Continuum 3. Mentoring

Place an X on the line to mark where your organisation is today, and date it.

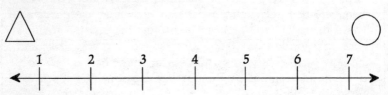

1	2	3	4	5	6	7

Telling
- Does not include everyone
- Based on efforts of a few
- In-house mentors only

Learning
- Everyone encouraged
- Formal programme exists
- Support exists for seeking mentors outside company

In the hierarchical organisation, someone with position and status becomes the mentor, offering a helping hand through project assistance, advice, networking and political support to a bright, talented newcomer in the company. The mentoring relationship thus becomes a significant source of learning for the younger, less-experienced person. As a result, his or her career often progresses faster than the norm.

In a learning organisation, these relationships are not left to chance. Individuals are actively recruited to mentor, and others are selected to be mentored. No one is left out of the process. Mentoring is used less for advancing someone's career than for advancing the learning process. Learning organisations recognise that in a successful mentoring relationship, the mentor learns as much as the person mentored. The content of mentoring goes beyond political and technical skills to the essence of how to learn. Additionally, mentoring can become a significant tool in creating the shared values of a learning culture.

How does mentoring occur in your company?

_____

_____

How could mentoring help your organisation become a learning organisation?

_____

_____

Continuum 4. On-the-job (OTJ) training

Place an X on the line to mark where your organisation is today, and date it.

Telling	Learning
• Formal induction for new employees	• Continuous commitment to growth
• Accidental and sporadic	• Planned
• Current position development only	• Cross-training encouraged
• No rewards for increased employee value	• Compensation for expanded skills
• Technical training only	• Develops reflection and enquiry

On the left end of the continuum, on-the-job training is confined to induction and technical training. Individuals usually receive this type of learning experience in the first few months of employment. If a new piece of equipment or technology is introduced, there may be another period of training to get people 'up and running'.

As the organisation moves towards the right end of the continuum, learning becomes fully integrated into the culture of the company and is valued for itself. Learning is integrated into meetings, work products and work processes. Time is routinely set aside to assess the learning from any given experience. Teams of people get together not just to solve problems or learn from mistakes, but to celebrate and learn from successes.

Cross-training – learning other jobs within the department or the company – is an element of OTJ training that is supported in learning organisations. It is often reinforced by the company by awarding higher pay to those who have learned more job skills. Cross-training increases the organisation's capacity to respond to changing customer needs. It provides the individual with an opportunity to continue growing.

OTJ learning is not limited just to technical skills, either. Reflection and enquiry, two interpersonal skills (known as 'soft' skills), are examples of the new ways OTJ training is being used today in learning organisations. Every aspect of the job becomes a potential opportunity for learning to use these skills.

Case study
Time for reflection

At the Ohio Manufacturers' Association, for example, reflection is integrated into their meetings. At the beginning of a meeting, participants are asked about what they've reflected on since the last meeting. This is a chance to raise issues, clarify points from the previous meetings, and share any learning that is relevant. At the close of the meeting, another five minutes or so are allocated to reflect on how productive the meeting was. This is not a time to rehash the content of the meeting, but rather to comment on how effectively it was run. Is there anything that might be reinforced, strengthened, repeated or deleted at the next meeting to make it more effective? In addition to the benefits of keeping the focus on learning, the reflection process has all but eliminated the 'meeting after the meeting' phenomenon.

Briefly describe how your company uses cross-training to enhance productivity and increase employee value to the company.

_____

_____

Excluding the training you received as a new employee, what on-the-job training have you participated in?

_____

_____

What does your company do to encourage learning at work?

_____

_____

Continuum 5. Staff development or learning plans
Place an X on the line to mark where your organisation is today, and date it.

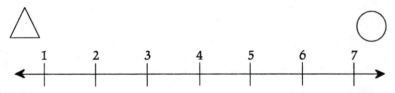

Telling
- Non-existent
- Required for accreditation
- Filed and reviewed perfunctorily for annual appraisals

Learning
- Initiated by individual learners or teams
- Funding available to fulfil plans
- Monitored by individual learners

On the left end of the continuum, staff development plans (when they exist) are instruments of control. Some organisations – hospitals, for instance – need these plans to maintain accreditation, and therefore they become a required part of the annual review process. Employee and manager both dread the process of filling in such development plans, and quickly learn how to take advantage of a few key phrases that sound good and don't mean much.

In moving towards the right end of the continuum, the training department may apply pressure on managers and employees to produce development plans. The intent is well-meaning: to have the individual plans provide meaningful data on the overall company training/learning needs. Sadly, both parties typically go through the process in a perfunctory way – the employee not thinking through learning goals; the supervisor identifying broad, vague objectives that can be used generically on all the forms that need to be filled in. In the end, the training department is perceived as creating more work, not as a resource for enhanced performance.

In a true learning organisàtion, the learning plan is an important document to everyone concerned. The individual assumes responsibility for his or her learning and creates a realistic written plan. The organisation budgets financial and time resources to support the plan. Because the individual understands the strategic vision, the individual learning goals will support the direction in which the organisation is moving.

Rather than a document for control, in a learning organisation the development plan becomes a tool for empowerment. If someone wants to attend a course in London in April, it isn't assumed that he or she is just trying to get a free holiday. There is trust that the proposed course is the best way to meet the identified need. The request of an employee for a specialised course available only at some distance would not be denied because management assumed the employee was interested only in the trip. For many employees, such as single parents, the trip may be a true inconvenience and personal strain, yet they volunteer to go knowing the course will meet their learning objectives. In the learning organisation, suspicion is replaced with trust as the organisation approaches the right end of the continuum.

What courses have you been denied because supervisors felt that your choice was not appropriate or relevant to your job?

_____

_____

_____

What positive steps does your organisation take to ensure that employee development plans are effective and realistic?

_____

_____

_____

List at least two classes or courses you would like to take and how you feel your organisation would benefit.

_____

_____

_____

Continuum 6. Teamwork

Place an X on the line to mark where your organisation is today, and date it.

Telling
- Non-existent, focus on individual
- Frustration is typical
- Knowledge is hoarded
- Focus on problems
- Exists only in some work groups

Learning
- Synergy in a team
- Sense of community
- Cross-discipline learning
- Focus on growth, success, improvement
- Team mates help one another to learn

31

In the telling organisation, teamwork is practically non-existent, or happens by accident. The competitive culture inhibits it. Focus is on individual star performers who compete for training perks. Those who are asked to serve on teams often feel they could do the task faster and more easily by themselves. They've heard about synergy, but they don't usually experience it.

The shift to teamwork (called self-directed teams in some organisations) as the preferred way of doing the work is extremely difficult, because it signifies a shift in the culture, values and norms of the company. The intent is for individuals to learn from one another, or as a team to go outside themselves for the expertise they need. To do this, groups of people need to learn the behaviour that will transform them into a team. Skills include problem-solving, facilitation, decision making, meeting management, conflict resolution, dialogue, enquiry and reflection. Team building is a step towards team learning, but does not yet describe a learning organisation.

Not surprisingly, team learning is the exception rather than the norm. In fact, many more companies are praising the benefits of teams than are creating real-life teams. In an effort to facilitate the transition to more teams, and potentially team learning, many experiments are being conducted. Here are just two.

1. A trainer and consultant in Columbus, Ohio, is changing the focus and methods used by teams. She is blending problem solving with studying achievements by creating success-oriented teams. Learning is enhanced through studying achievements, not just failures.

2. A consultant in St Petersburg, Florida, has created esteem teams. These are groups of people within companies that are committed to personal learning and development. They meet weekly and use an audio programme as the basis of their learning and development. Each week a different group member leads the discussion. The purpose is to direct their personal learning towards organisational learning.

Describe how teamwork is being used in your company.

_____

_____

_____

_____

Give an example of team learning that you've observed or experienced.

_____

_____

_____

_____

List some of the successes your teams have experienced.

_____

_____

_____

_____

Continuum 7. Benchmarking
Place an X on the line to mark where your organisation is today, and date it.

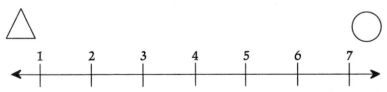

Telling
- Jockeying to position a department, division or team as 'the best' to increase power
- Little or no recognition of excellence

Learning
- Identifying excellence within the company and sharing it for new applications in other parts of the company
- Identifying excellence in other companies or industries as an incentive for growth

On the left end of the continuum, benchmarking (if it is used at all) is a tool of control, used to force a department to increase its productivity or effectiveness.

In a learning organisation, the benchmarking process helps teams or work groups to look outside themselves to identify learning opportunities. To establish benchmarks, a team identifies another company in the industry or another team in the company that is perceived to be outstanding at what it does. Then the team studies that organisation/team, perhaps making on-site visits and doing interviews with key individuals. Based on the data collected, the team looks for ways to learn from the other company/team's experience, and in the process how it can advance.

Wausau Insurance Company is an example of one company that is using benchmarking to increase its performance. Project leader and internal consultant Ron Laconi has said, 'While it's good to compare ourselves from within ... we also need to look at our competitors who have a reputation as being the best within the insurance industry. For example, we want people to be as satisfied with our billing process as they are with American Express, because American Express has consistently demonstrated its leadership in this area.'*

Continuum 8. Partnership
Place an X on the line to mark where your organisation is today, and date it.

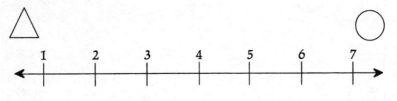

---

* Ford, Susan. 'You Can Teach an Old Dog New Tricks.' *Good People*. Employers Insurance of Wausau: Wausau, Wisconsin, November 1994, p 5.

Telling	Learning
● Rare	● Established with customers, suppliers, co-workers, vendors
● Used to transfer technical skills from manufacturer to distributor, or from distributor to customer	● Expands beyond technical skills to business and 'soft' skills
● Emphasis on competition	● Increases cooperation
● Short-term relationship based on lowest price	● Long-term relationship based on quality products

The concept of partnership has only recently been understood outside a legal agreement or personal relationship. The learning organisation recognises partnership as significant in learning and long-term success. Today there are partnerships with customers, suppliers and even competitors.

Case study
Creating a learning partnership

General Electric Appliances is one example of a company that has created a learning partnership with its customers. General Electric (US) produces major appliances that are sold to retail appliance dealers, who then make them available to individual consumers.

In 1992, the company decided to learn more about the world through the eyes of its distributors, and discovered that many of their dealers were small family businesses struggling to survive. Armed with this information, General Electric Appliances set out to share its learning with its dealers. The firm produced a book for its dealers, titled *Major Appliance Retailing*, designed to help retailers run their small businesses more successfully.

It proved to be the first step in an ongoing learning partnership. What used to be an us/them relationship has become one of working together to achieve mutual goals. Now many of the retailers are consulting a General Electric representative about their retail account plans. And as General Electric continues to learn from its customers, the firm gets better at meeting its customers' needs.

Exercise
Assess your organisation

You can assess your overall progress towards becoming a learning organisation by adding together your score on each of the tools' continuums. If your total score is 24 or less, you're still functioning primarily as a traditional hierarchical, pyramid organisation. A score between 25 and 40 indicates that your organisation is in transition. A score of 41 or higher suggests that you've made significant progress towards becoming a learning organisation. In the space below, record your score today. Come back at six-month intervals, reassess your organisation on each continuum, and note the progress you've made.

	DATE	SCORE	DATE	SCORE	DATE	SCORE
Tuition reimbursement	___	___	___	___	___	___
Formal training	___	___	___	___	___	___
Mentoring	___	___	___	___	___	___
OTJ training						
Development/Learning plans	___	___	___	___	___	___
Teamwork	___	___	___	___	___	___
Benchmarking	___	___	___	___	___	___
Partnership	___	___	___	___	___	___
Total score	___		___		___	

Getting – and keeping – the learning edge

If your company is financially strong and morale is high, it is easy to slip into what we call *learning arrogance*. Obviously, you know how to do things and do them well. Witness your success! But rather than become a learning organisation, you may be focused on being a telling organisation – telling others how great you are and telling your employees what to do. So why would your business need to learn more, or learn from anyone else?

The reason is, everything changes. And in today's world, the changes are occurring at an amazing speed. In the 1960s, Andy Warhol said we'd each have 15 minutes of fame sometime in our life. Businesses are no exception to this prediction. If your organisation is having its moment in the limelight, don't make the mistake of thinking you have arrived. Learn from IBM and remember how fast 15 minutes passes.

When your group is at the peak is the time when you are most vulnerable. Success can blind you. The challenge is to realise that when you've reached a peak, you're really at the crest of a curve, and the next natural move is downward. This is the moment to become proactive and look for the next learning challenge. Take advantage of where you are, and let today's success be the foundation for moving into areas less known. Consider the Microsoft organisation: Are they working today on more software packages for computers? No, they're making plans to enter your home with 'edutainment', home shopping and interactive television. Chairman Bill Gates is not letting Microsoft become learning arrogant, but is instead keeping his company on the learning edge.

CHAPTER 3
The Organisation's Responsibility for Learning

Organisational attitudes to learning

Learning is an individual responsibility, yet an organisation can go a long way towards providing an environment that supports and encourages individual learning. Young children who have an environment rich in stimuli – colours, shapes, textures, tastes – learn more than children who lack this environmental support. It is the same for organisations and their adult learners.

Knowing that learning will give the competitive edge, it's hard to imagine any company not wanting to maximise its support of learning. Here are some of the things that you can do to make your company 'learner friendly'.

Invest the time

How much time will you give your employees to learn? If we were talking about money, the typical rule of thumb is to invest 10 per cent in your future through savings. That's not a bad guideline for learning, either. Are you willing to invest 10 per cent of your employees' time in learning? Ideally, this will happen on a regular, daily basis as opposed to once or twice a year. Why is regularity so important? It gets employees into the learning habit. As they become oriented to learning in every situation, you can influence the learning. It becomes cumulative, and takes learning out of the realm of an event and into a regular process.

Include learning in your culture and values

It's easy to talk about having a commitment to learning, but what of your corporate culture and corporate values? What is really considered important? Do top managers 'send employees to training' while staying behind, immersed in their daily tasks? In her seminars, your author has heard many people say, 'You know who needs to hear this message? My manager.' If training and learning are considered necessary only for the rank and file, and not for everyone, the organisation is not sending a message that learning is valued. The opposite condition, too, is detrimental. Consider the case study below.

Case study
Learning is for everyone

In a recent seminar, a secretary attended along with supervisors and managers. After the programme she was filled with enthusiasm. She had worked in the organisation for eight years, but this was the first training programme she had ever attended. She loved the learning and said, 'I wish I could go to more courses'.

This organisation spent training money only on its 'professional' staff. Unfortunately, it did not consider its secretarial staff as professional, and was losing the commitment to learning it might have received from its 'non-professional' staff.

Review

Take a few minutes now to jot down your organisation's values about learning and training.

_____

_____

Are learning opportunities provided for everyone, or only a special group?

_____

_____

Do all individuals have equal access to learning? What are the opportunities?

_____

_____

Is learning a perk, a punishment or a routine part of the job?

_____

_____

Provide space for learning

How are your offices laid out? Do people live in cubicles? Are conversations and meetings held behind closed doors? Where are meetings and projects conducted?

It's difficult to learn about the work of others if you don't regularly see them or the work they're doing. Herman Miller, an office furniture manufacturer, asks prospective customers to describe how their work gets done. Based on the answers to this question, furniture is designed for three different styles of teamwork.

Style 1. Linear teams

Linear teams perform routine, repetitive tasks that are passed from one person to the next until the process is complete and it moves to the next team. Examples of linear teams are stock control and loan processing. Although meetings do occur to discuss the work, individuals work independently most of the day at their own desks. There is limited learning outside of technical skills.

Offices are next to each other, so work can be passed from one to the next. There is lots of privacy because work is done independently.

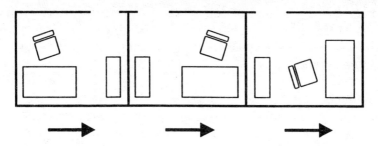

Offices for linear teams

Style 2. Parallel teams

Parallel teams consist of people with specialised skills essential to achieving project outcomes. Most employees serve on several teams. Parallel teams need meeting space as well as private space. Often, project-related materials need to be kept accessible to all team members. More cross-training and shared knowledge are needed than in a linear team. To facilitate this, the space is designed with many formal and informal meeting spaces, and open offices.

Office space for parallel teams

Style 3. Circular teams

In circular teams, there is the greatest demand for open space and easy communication among team members. Learning is

41

maximised in these democratic teams. Creativity and brainstorming are significant parts of the work, so office spaces use bulletin boards or open walls on which ideas are collected and added to.

According to *The Wall Street Journal*, executives at the Aluminum Company of America have recently moved out of their executive suites and into a cluster of cockpit-style offices. The L-shaped desks and tables for small, impromptu meetings have made decision making faster and increased interaction and learning.

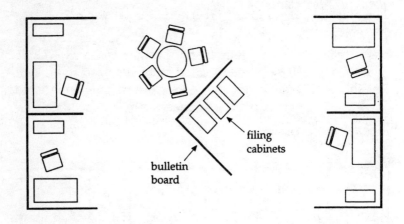

Office space for circular teams

How is your organisation using space to facilitate learning?

_____

_____

How does the space promote or inhibit collaboration?

_____

_____

How does the space encourage people to build on the ideas of others?

_____

_____

What physical barriers to learning exist?

_____

_____

How does the space support the current technologies needed to do the work?

_____

_____

How have private offices been arranged to encourage informal discussion and problem solving?

_____

_____

Does your physical layout and furniture assume equal access to information, ideas and people?

_____

_____

Respond to learning mistakes

In the typical organisation, a mistake can result in damage to a person's self-esteem, a lower salary increase or a lost promotion. It is the _atypical_ company that treats mistakes as a learning opportunity. In today's environment, businesses need people who are willing to take risks and show initiative. That means errors will be made. How your organisation responds to a mistake is crucial, because mistakes can lead to knowledge. Don't sacrifice learning to the expediency of 'fixing the mistake', 'searching for the guilty' and 'damage control'. Instead, allow each error to become a learning opportunity.

This isn't to imply that you won't need corrective action following an error. To benefit from the error, however, the organisation needs to be willing to stop and reflect on what happened and why.

- What can be done differently in the future to prevent the mistake recurring?
- Does the mistake have implications for any other projects or departments in the company?
- Who else in the company could benefit from the learning if it were shared?
- How have the individuals involved grown as a result of the mistake?

An error says, 'Take time for reflection', not, 'Make a judgement'. With this approach, the company can increase its overall capacity to learn. Stay focused on improving the process, not on looking for someone to blame.

What happens in your company when a mistake is made?

_____

_____

_____

_____

Adopt proactive versus retrospective learning
Learning from mistakes is an example of retrospective learning. In other words, the employee learns something after an event has taken place. Often, the event that provokes the learning is negative – an outright mistake, or perhaps a disappointing or unexpected outcome. Although it's less common, learning from past success is also retrospective learning, and is certainly more motivating.

Unfortunately, with most retrospective learning the essence of what is learned is that the outcome didn't meet expectations or was unpleasant. In these circumstances, people don't necessarily take the next step to change their behaviour the next time they are in a similar situation. Further, retrospective learning is by chance. Even if an outcome doesn't meet expectations, that is no guarantee that learning will take place. Perhaps it isn't true that experience is the best teacher!

Something happens ➡ **Maybe you reflect** ➡ **Maybe you learn**

When the learning experience is planned, however, that is the heart of *proactive learning*. In this type of learning, the individual sets a specific and personal learning goal, deciding at the outset what learning is desired. That is not to say that some unexpected or unanticipated learning won't occur, but when a plan exists and there is intent to learn, experience is always an excellent teacher. People will miss out on significant learning opportunities when they enter experiences with no plan to learn, and they will leave these experiences without reflecting upon what was gained. Until learning is a focus of attention in every experience, the organisation will miss opportunities to integrate and internalise learning into the corporate culture.

Plan to learn ➡ **Experience** ➡ **You learn**

Imagine that you are preparing to go to an annual professional conference. How could you plan, proactively, for what you want to learn? Compare your list with the one that follows, which was drawn up by a training director.

_____

_____

_____

_____

What I'll learn at the next annual conference
1. Networking skills, by meeting industry people I want to know
2. What training styles are most effective
3. What training technologies are being used by other companies in my industry
4. How to use humour in my training programmes
5. How to select trainers for a programme
6. What books other trainers are reading that are influencing their work
7. Industry trends since the last meeting
8. One new idea to help us move towards becoming a learning organisation

Suppose one of the objectives embedded in all your organisation's work was, 'What can I learn as a result of doing this work?' This mind-set would make everyone a proactive learner. What kind of impact would it make in your company?

Treat work like practice
Work can be an opportunity to practise what you've learned and what you are learning. In fact, many professionals call their work just that, a practice. Physicians have medical practices, lawyers practise law. Therapists and counsellors have private practices. The assumption behind this is that they are still learning, still searching for truth. The common thread throughout all these professions is that learning is the

foundation for what they do. The more they practise, the more learning they do, and the better they get. What would happen if people thought of themselves as going to practise each day rather than to work? Would it restore some of the fun and curiosity? Would it reduce the pressure to know it all, or save face by pretending you do?

Reward employees for learning

The premise of Michael LeBoeuf's best-selling book, *The Greatest Management Principle in the World*, is that behaviour that is rewarded is repeated. Why not apply that principle to learning? If you want your employees to be committed to lifelong learning, reward them for learning.*

A learning quick check

There are many creative ways to reward employees for learning. In the following list, tick the items that your company already uses.

- ☐ Certificates of achievement for classes taken
- ☐ Articles in the company newsletter about learning experiences
- ☐ Cash awarded for competencies acquired
- ☐ Recognition at company-wide meetings
- ☐ Verbal recognition at the time of learning
- ☐ Awards given for team learning achievements
- ☐ Awards given for individual learning achievements
- ☐ Allocated time at management or team meetings to describe learning experiences
- ☐ Integration of learning into performance appraisals

- ☐ _____
- ☐ _____

---

* Michael LeBoeuf, *The Greatest Management Principle in the World*. London: Sidgwick and Jackson, 1986.

Organisation structure

If someone in your company attends a training programme or reads a book and is stimulated to try doing things a different way, what happens? Is he or she encouraged to suggest and experiment, or is he or she told, 'That's fine for the class or as a theory in a book, but this is the way we do things here'?

Some companies are organised into functional units popularly called silos. In such organisations, the structure itself gets in the way of communication between functional areas. Different departments of the same company may actually pay different prices for the same service from the same vendor. Without a structure that encourages shared learning, learning is isolated to a particular functional unit. The organisation pays dearly when learning is localised and not dispersed.

How does your organisation ensure that learning is shared across departments?

Political environment

In many organisations, power is vested heavily in a few individuals. The rest of the organisation spends its energy learning to identify the 'pet projects' and key values of those in power. The staff assume that the more effectively they play this game, the brighter their career outlook will be. Many employees are consumed by trying to ferret out the desires of those they perceive as powerful. And learning, like any other company objective, may be 'on the agenda' or 'off the agenda' of those in power.

This political game is acutely visible in government. Newly elected officials may come in with an agenda that complements or completely undoes the previous office holders' work. In one training programme offered to a US state government agency, employees said that in their 15 years of service, they'd been through six different administrations. The employees' tenure had outlasted all the officials', and the employees continued doing things the way they wanted to do them. Training was endured, not implemented.

Barriers to learning

As much as learning wants to flow through the organisation, it often gets blocked. One of the most important things your organisation can do is to actively look for the barriers that inhibit learning or slow it down. Then take steps to remove the obstacles. Here are some of the most common ones.

Mixed messages
When your organisation's words and behaviour don't agree, you are sending a mixed message. For example, your company may state a policy that learning is important and may encourage people to attend training. At the same time, however, individuals may still be expected to do their regular work on the days that they attend training. This probably means they have to come in early or work late. It may require them to go back to their desks during lunch, or that when they return from training, the previous day's work is still waiting for them. They're getting a mixed message from your company about the value of learning.

When faced with a mixed message, most people believe the behaviour rather than the words. When you send a mixed message about learning, you undermine your objective to become a learning organisation.

What mixed messages do you receive? What could be done to improve the situation?

_____

_____

Lack of resources
Among training and development professionals, it's a widely made assumption that in the face of financial pressures, the first

thing to get cut will be training. As you move towards becoming a learning organisation, there is no guarantee that your company will not encounter difficult choices in the face of lean times.

What has been your organisation's commitment to learning when money is tight?

Businesses may also be victims of fluctuating priorities, especially with today's rate of change among managing directors and chairmen. At a resort, the MD was deeply committed to training and to developing a learning organisation. Employees attended many training programmes, and had raised expectations of being involved in company decisions and communication. When the resort experienced financial difficulties, a new chairman was hired — one who focused not on the development of employees, but on the bottom line. Five years later, yet another new chairman was on the scene, and again committed to training. Not surprisingly, the employees are taking a 'wait and see' attitude.

How have politics affected the learning agenda in your organisation?

Unclear, conflicting, or missing vision

A vision provides direction to an organisation and its employees. It helps to clarify what is important. Without a vision, or with one that is unclear, it is difficult to know what needs to be learned. The organisation that tells its employees they are responsible for their learning without giving them a context for that learning does them a disservice. For instance, an art class might be appropriate for someone who will be using desktop publishing in his or her work. If, however, the organisation plans to outsource its newsletter and other company publications, that art class may be irrelevant.

Can you write out the mission and vision of your organisation without 'looking it up'?

_____

_____

Managing organisational learning

Perhaps the greatest challenge in creating a learning organisation is to see that the learning flows into every nook and cranny of the business. It's one thing to offer courses or send people on seminars, and even to be certain that the training is well delivered and customised to your organisation's needs. But how do you manage the actual implementation of the learning? How do you support and facilitate the application of knowledge so that true learning does occur? And how do you make sure this is happening across an organisation of diverse people, perhaps diverse locations, among jobs with differing demands and constraints? In this section, we shall attempt to shed some light on these questions.

Three styles of learning
Style 1. Spontaneous learning
Learning goes on all the time in greater or lesser degrees. Sometimes the learning is _spontaneous_ to the project or task at hand. For example, as you're filling a box with product to be sent to a customer, you learn how to pack the box most efficiently. You learn that by the way you place the items in the box, you can increase the number shipped from 18 to 20.

Write an example of spontaneous learning that you've experienced or observed at your company.

_____

_____

Style 2. Accidental learning

Accidental learning occurs as an unexpected outcome of a situation. Imagine you're in a meeting where someone is angry and starts to shout at the chairperson. The chairperson does not appear to be upset or defensive, but instead calmly reflects the person's feelings, restores control to the meeting and continues with the agenda. Later, during the same meeting, anger is directed at you. You're surprised to find yourself responding with the same kind of composure the chairperson displayed. You did not go to the meeting planning to learn how to handle an angry person; nor was that the content of the meeting. By accident, you learned this productive way to handle the situation.

Unfortunately, not all accidental learning is positive. Using the previous example, it's just as likely that you could learn to shout right back and attempt to intimidate others when they want something.

List examples of accidental learning that you've experienced or observed.

_____

_____

_____

Passive learning. In accidental and spontaneous learning, the learner does not make a conscious decision to learn. The learning was not proactive. Rather, it happened unintentionally and was an outcome of experience. This passive approach to learning is how most people say they learn. They think they are learning all the time. Therefore, why pay any special attention to learning?

The goal in getting an individual to focus and direct his or her efforts towards learning is to increase the probability that that person will experience spontaneous and accidental learning. When awareness of learning is raised, people become more attuned to learning opportunities. They see what was always there but may have been overlooked.

Analogy. Think about the last new car you bought. Like many people, before you bought your car you probably didn't pay much attention to your particular make, model, or colour of car on the road. Suddenly, though, after you buy it, you see your new car everywhere!

For individuals to increase their spontaneous and accidental learning, they need to increase their *planned* learning.

Style 3. Planned learning
In contrast to the other two styles of learning, *planned learning* is conscious. It is a goal purposefully set. It can happen in a classroom or on the job. It can happen with a customer, a vendor, a co-worker or a box. The critical variable is that learning is the desired result. An individual goes into the situation with the intention to learn, to be proactive.

One key to creating a learning organisation is to increase the emphasis and commitment to planned learning, rather than trusting that it will happen on its own. When some forethought has been given to what needs to be learned from a situation or experience, learning can occur in nearly any context.

Jot down the ways in which your company currently encourages planned learning.

_____

_____

_____

Exercise
Planned learning
Imagine that you work in a social service agency. Some of your routine tasks are listed below. Write down possible learning opportunities that you see in these routine tasks. To get you started, one possible idea is listed for each task.

TASK: **Attend meetings with community members**
LEARNING:

Learn how to influence community leaders in meetings

TASK: **Be in charge of five major projects**
LEARNING:

Learn how to manage multiple priorities

TASK: **Be an agency spokesperson during times of community crisis**
LEARNING:

Learn how to communicate effectively with the public through the media

---

TASK: **Supervise a staff of eight**
LEARNING:

Practise giving feedback that is specific

Think about the increased learning potential for your company if, during the hiring process and induction period, new employees were asked to set learning objectives for the key components of their job. As they gained experience on the job, they could influence those objectives by sharing them with their work group or team. In this way, learning would become more integrated into the work itself, and not seen as something extra to be added on.

Determine what type of learning is needed

Just as learning can occur in different ways, there are different types of learning. As you improve the opportunities for planned learning to occur, you may begin to consider what type of learning will move your organisation most efficiently towards the desired outcomes. In this section we shall examine beginner's learning, incremental learning, unlearning, and transformational learning.

First learning

Perhaps individuals know nothing about what needs to be learned. In this case, you facilitate *first learning* — or what is called *Beginner's Mind* in Zen meditation practice. You invite people to enter the learning experience with an open mind; to have no expectations or preconceived ideas. Shunryu Suzuki says,* in *Zen Mind, Beginner's Mind*, 'In the beginner's mind there are many possibilities, but in the expert's there are few.' Most training programmes would be more successful if learners entered the classroom with Beginner's Mind.

Incremental learning

When you want to build on existing strengths and skills, you need *incremental learning*, in which a skill is refined over time. For example, a manager who gives presentations may be, in general, quite effective. However, the manager could have more impact with a stronger closing statement. Incremental

---

* Shunryu Suzuki, *Zen Mind, Beginner's Mind*. London: Weatherhill, 1973.

learning for this manager would involve adding to other presentation skills the ability to make concise summaries.

Enhancing or expanding a skill is also incremental learning. For example, consider a group of salespeople who have mastered the selling process. You want them to integrate more customer service after each sale. This is another example of incremental learning.

Unlearning

Increasingly, the task for employees is not to add to what they already know or to learn something new, but to *unlearn* what they know. This is especially true in technological fields. With a new release of a computer program, for example, some incremental learning may be required. But another significant requirement may be to unlearn the old version. For example, a 'Print' command key in one version of the program may have been changed to mean 'Save to Disk' in the new version. You need to 'forget' what you knew in order to be open to remembering the new information.

Many people are reluctant to unlearn what they know. How often have you heard the phrase, 'We've always done it this way', or 'If it ain't broke, don't fix it'? These phrases reflect a desire to maintain the status quo. In incremental learning, you keep your current learning and body of knowledge and add to it in some way. In unlearning, what you have done and known before becomes obsolete and is dropped to make room for something new.

Zen and the art of learning

There is a wonderful Zen story that describes why we sometimes need to empty ourselves first, before we can learn. A university professor went to visit a Zen master at a temple in Japan. As he was seated for tea with the master, the professor began talking. On and on he went, without a pause. As he spoke, the master poured tea. Suddenly the professor jumped up, realising that the tea had overflowed the cup, the saucer, and was now in his lap. Yet still the master poured.

'Stop! What are you doing?!' The master looked up and said, 'Just as the cup can hold no more tea when it is full, how can I teach you when your mind is already full?'

Transformational learning

The last type of learning is called a *paradigm shift* or *transformational learning*. This is the most powerful of all the types of learning, because it shifts a person's point of view on the world. As a consequence, a paradigm shift is often followed by a cascade of unlearning and incremental learning. Some organisations refer to this type of learning as *culture change*.

A paradigm shift is profound and can happen in a flash. There is a moment of 'Aha!' when the individual 'gets it' and suddenly sees things in a different way. The new paradigm transforms their world view in a significant way. Interestingly enough, a paradigm shift often involves seeing what was previously true as false, or what was false as true.

Here are some examples of paradigm shifts:

- You see your customer instead of your boss as the centre of your business.
- Your boss sees his or her job as that of serving you rather than controlling you.
- You become partners with your competitors.
- You change from 'having a job' to 'doing meaningful work'.
- The organisation shifts from being a series of functional parts to being an integrated whole.
- The focus of an organisation or individual shifts from solving problems to achieving successful solutions.

What paradigm shifts are occurring at your company?

_____

_____

Reflect on the learning that is most needed in your organisation right now. Does it need first learning, incremental learning, unlearning or transformational learning?_____

Developing resources – and resourcefulness – in learning

In a learning organisation, the training department is not the primary source of learning experiences or opportunities. That is too narrow and too shortsighted. Instead, the whole body of work, every person in the organisation, and every project all become potential sites for learning. Even competitors, suppliers and customers can be resources for learning. The challenge is to *identify and access these learning resources.*

In planned learning, you take time to think through what needs to be learned. From whom or what can it best be learned? What is the time frame in which it needs to be learned? Will a formal educational course be necessary? Is there a book, video, or audio programme that will meet the need?

Imagine for a moment that you need to learn the following things. What resources would you tap in your organisation?

- How to negotiate with a supplier for a product you need.
  Learning resources: _____

- How to resolve a conflict with a co-worker.
  Learning resources: _____

- How to write a better business letter.
  Learning resources: _____

- How to be less judgemental during meetings.
  Learning resources: _____

- How to engage the support of others for a project you're working on.
  Learning resources: _____

It may happen that an individual will complain, 'My boss is incompetent. I can't learn anything from him/her. I'm stuck in a dead end here.' That is a very narrow view, in which the boss is the only identified learning resource. Don't let anyone fall into this trap! It's important to help everyone see the full range of learning resources available to them.

Now that we've covered the aspects of your organisation's responsibility for creating a climate conducive to learning, we shall turn our attention to the responsibilities of an individual for learning and personal mastery.

CHAPTER 4
The Individual's Responsibility for Learning

Attitudes to cultivate in individual learners

In any organisation there are three types of learner. These types can be placed on a continuum just as the organisational tools were in Chapter 2. At the left end are reluctant learners, people whose learning took place in the past. At the right end are lifelong learners, people who look to the future and decide what they need to learn today. And in the middle are leisurely learners, people with a focus on the present: 'What do I need to learn right now to do my job?'

Read the following descriptions of each type of learner, and decide which type of learner you are.

Reluctant learners
Motto: Been There, Done That
- Resist learning anything new
- Regardless of education level, they feel they've already been to school
- Cling to the security of what they know
- See no need for further learning
- Live by phrases such as, 'Can't teach an old dog new tricks'
- Whine that they don't get promoted

- Don't get the interesting assignments
- Are the first ones laid off when there is downsizing.

In a class or a training programme, these are the people sitting in the back of the room, rolling their eyes, and talking to their neighbours or working on something other than the course work. Reluctant learners can be a liability to your organisation. Some may have been with the company for ten years, yet have gained only one year of experience ten times over.

Leisurely learners
Motto: This Too Shall Pass
- Keep up with the required training to meet current expectations
- And that's about all they do: the minimum expected
- Sometimes complain, other times enjoy learning
- Don't volunteer for new assignments or ask to attend training programmes
- Do what is recommended or required by their boss
- See teams as an opportunity to sit back and relax
- Many are successful because they know how to play the political games.

In today's environment, they feel threatened and genuinely confused about all the changing expectations. The leisurely learner may become a reluctant learner if he or she is punished for learning, discouraged from learning, or encounters other organisation barriers to learning.

Lifelong learners
Motto: If It's New, Try It
- Volunteer to attend learning events
- Read relevant books and professional magazines
- Talk to lots of people about what they're doing and how they're learning
- Watch for and anticipate the trends
- Prepare themselves to leap into the future
- Experiment with new ideas.

Lifelong learners may have years of experience and be highly respected by their colleagues, yet they're always taking notes and drinking in new ideas. These are the people you want to cultivate and nurture in your organisation.

In reality, we are all a little of each type of learner *in some area*. Each of us has a primary learning attitude, but with a little reflection, you can probably identify some area of learning that is not your main learning style. After reading the previous descriptions of learning attitudes, you have probably identified your basic attitude towards learning. Now work through the following exercise to identify areas of learning that may not be your main style.

Exercise
Learning styles identification
On the continuum below, list at least five examples for each category of learning attitude. These can be personal or work-related areas. What are you reluctant to learn? What do you learn because it's required? What are you learning to prepare yourself for the future? To get you started, a few examples are listed.

PAST	PRESENT	FUTURE
← RELUCTANT	LEISURELY	LIFELONG →
Operate new equipment	Learn new software	Hobby
New exercise regimen	Time management techniques	Management skills

In some areas your attitude is that of a lifelong learner, while in other areas you are a reluctant learner. What seems to make the difference? We shall explore this question later.

Now let's take a look at what sets lifelong learners apart from the rest. The first difference is their attitude about mistakes.

Lifelong learners follow up on their mistakes
What do you do when you make a mistake? You can choose how to respond. Read through the following simple example and examine the different possibilities listed for responding to this error. Tick the ones you would have used in the past.

You have just introduced the guest speaker at your company's annual general meeting. Afterwards, the speaker tells you that you mispronounced her name. What is your response?

- ☐ **1.** I said it right.
- ☐ **2.** The paper didn't say how to pronounce it.
- ☐ **3.** I said it the way you told me to.
- ☐ **4.** I didn't think anyone would notice.
- ☐ **5.** Oh, how *do* you pronounce your name?

Now let's see what each of these responses represents.

- Statement 1 is an example of *denial*. In this case no learning takes place and you've created a potential conflict with the speaker.
- Statement 2 is an example of *defensiveness*. You have read a written, prepared introduction that didn't specify the pronunciation, so how can it be your fault? Still no learning takes place here, either.
- Statement 3 is an example of *blaming others* when a mistake is made. In this case, you've *certainly* aroused defensiveness in the speaker. Still no learning occurs.
- Statement 4 is an example of *trying to conceal* your mistake. You have erroneously assumed that if no one knows about it, it didn't really happen. Again, no learning occurs

- With statement 5 there is an acknowledgement of the mistake and a statement of the desire to learn. A mistake is a trigger for learning — without making mistakes, you're just playing it safe and not growing or risking anything.

What is your typical reaction when you make a mistake?

_____

_____

_____

Equally important, how do you respond when a mistake is made by someone else? Do you blame? Judge? Criticise? Or do you help the other person to learn from the mistake?

_____

_____

_____

In many organisations mistakes are concealed because the consequence for making one is so negative. How does your organisation treat a person who makes a mistake?

_____

_____

_____

The stages of learning

The lifelong learner isn't afraid to use these three magic words: '*I don't know.*' To people who want to learn, these words are empowering. If they don't know the answer, they can ask questions and seek out the answer. Too often, people are reluctant to use the magic words, fearing that they will be perceived as inadequate or incompetent.

Stage 1. Unconscious incompetent

As you learn, you pass through stages of competence, as
identified by William Howell in his book *Empathic Communications*. The first stage is *unconscious incompetent.** At this
stage you don't know that you don't know, as in the
expression, 'What you don't know won't hurt you.' In some
respects this is a naive and blissful state, because there is no
discomfort about not knowing something. For example,
consider the manager who has just taken a job in a new
company. She knows from the interview that the company is
immersed in implementing a quality programme, but she's
never been exposed to what this means in day-to-day work.
She's always tried to do quality work and can't imagine that
this will be much different. This manager is an unconscious
incompetent, knowing nothing of what will be required of her
in her new job.

Stage 2. Conscious incompetent

It doesn't take long for the new manager to move to the
second stage: *conscious incompetent*. At this point, she *knows* she
doesn't know. This is a time characterised by stress, sometimes
disillusionment, and a significant opportunity to use the three
magic words: 'I don't know.' She's moved from the blissful
ignorance state to a state of discomfort (at times extreme
discomfort!). Now the manager is on the so-called *learning
curve*. When she attends meetings, people talk about
opportunity analysis, cause and effect matrix, and PERT
charts. She is acutely aware that she doesn't know what these
words mean, or how to use these quality tools. Her early
attempts to apply the tools result in confusion and frustration.

Stage 3. Conscious competent

As the weeks pass, the manager asks questions, practises using
the quality tools and gradually achieves the stage of *conscious*

---

* William Howell, *Empathic Communications*, Belmont, California:
  Wadsworth, 1982.

competent. She begins to understand which tools to use in which situations. She knows how to use each of the tools effectively. She stops worrying that she'll embarrass herself in a meeting because she doesn't know the difference between a PERT chart and a Gantt chart. At this stage, using the tools still demands concentration. But there is less stress, more fun, and a growing sense of pride in her new knowledge and skills. Discomfort begins its transformation into comfort.

Stage 4. Unconscious competent

Continued practice gets the learner to the fourth stage: *unconscious competent.* At this point the manager no longer needs to check a reference manual for how to use a specific quality tool. She doesn't need to analyse which tool to use in a given situation. Using the tools has become enjoyable. What a wonderful place to reach! The skill has not only become familiar; it has become a reflex action. But there are risks to this stage of unconscious competence.

Risk 1. Learning arrogance

When you've worked diligently to learn a skill and practised long and hard to become efficient at it, you are more likely to resist new ways of accomplishing that task. For instance, our manager is visited by a vendor one day, who suggests that there is a special computer and software package that will enable a team to make faster, wiser decisions. The vendor is convinced that the new technology is an advance over the quality tools the manager currently uses. But the manager is comfortable with her quality tools. Whether objections to innovation are verbalised or not, the message conveyed is, 'My way is best.' When the unconscious competent is experiencing success with one way, she may not be open to another way. Have you ever seen this happen?

Risk 2. Boredom

When you can do the job without thinking about it, where is the challenge? Where is the excitement? Ironically, a person at this advanced stage of learning can become a liability for an organisation because she loses some motivation, has time to complain, and may resist new ways of doing things.

What's the solution to the pitfalls of unconscious competence? One answer is to begin a learning cycle again in a new area, or with a new skill. This is one of the benefits of job rotation and cross-training. Learners re-enter the unconscious incompetent stage, which invites ongoing learning. another solution is proposed by Bob Pike in his book, *Creative Training Techniques Handbook*.* He suggests there is a fifth stage — conscious unconscious competent — which involves teaching others how to do what you do. This, of course, is one of the reasons learning organisations begin using internal trainers instead of relying only on the training department or outside experts. Teaching is one of the quickest ways to learn. Everyone can become a mentor in some area, which strengthens teamwork and cooperation.

Stage 5. Mastery

There is yet another stage of learning: *mastery*. George Leonard, author of *Mastery*,† says that as a person learns, there are spurts of growth followed by a plateau. Early in the learning process, the spurts of growth are closer together and there's a sense of accomplishment. However, the time spent on the plateau grows longer as the climb becomes steeper and the refinements more subtle. Leonard uses *aikido*, a Japanese martial art based on joint locks and throws, as his analogy. Many people begin a martial art and enjoy the first year or so of classes when learning is most rapid. But then they stop coming to classes. They never earn their black belt. That's because most people, particularly in Western cultures, enjoy the feeling that is associated with the growth spurt. They start new projects and experience that initial thrill of learning and accomplishment. But as soon as the learning slows down and

---

* Robert Pike, *Creative Training Techniques Handbook*. Minneapolis, Minnesota: Lakewood Books, 1994.
† George Leonard, *Mastery*. New York: Plume, 1992.

becomes more subtle, they tire of the project and turn their attention to something new. People often don't stay with one thing long enough to truly master it.

Think of each of the learning stages as a plateau. Some people won't stick with learning something long enough to master it, to reach that final stage. Mastery is a process and not an endpoint to be reached. The challenge is to learn to love the plateau since that is where you spend the major part of your life.

The growth spurts are peaks, moments that are not sustained. They motivate you to continue practising on the plateau, knowing that eventually you'll move from this plateau to another.

The process of mastering something requires both time and commitment. A meditation teacher once said, 'If you insist on evaluating your practice, do it only at ten-year intervals'. Yet we want our companies to show profits and growth on a quarterly basis! That short-term mind-set is in direct contradiction to the process of learning. Mastery as an approach to learning and running our organisations represents transformation – another paradigm shift.

Examine your own learned skills
Take a few minutes now to apply these concepts to your working life. Think of something that you've learned and have taken from the stage of unconscious incompetence toward mastery.

Give examples of skills that you've developed as far as conscious competence.

_____

_____

_____

Give an example of a skill that you are now teaching to others (mentoring).

_____

_____

_____

What are you currently practising that you would like to master?

_____

_____

_____

Openness to learning

The lifelong learner keeps an open mind to learning. It is a significant accomplishment to do this and avoid learning arrogance and the tendency to judge. How does one stay open? Here are some tips.

- **Surrender.** At its simplest, this is acknowledging that you don't know. You surrender to the teacher, to the process or to the task to learn. Surrender can happen early, when something is brand new, and it can happen when you're well on the way towards mastery.
- **Be curious.** This is a stage common to children, especially young children, in which the world is filled with wonder. As a learner, you want to understand and experience the wonder. This feeling state takes you outside yourself, and focuses you on the object or subject about which you feel curious.
- **Have intent or purpose.** Approach life with the intention to learn. Believe that part of your purpose in each activity, interaction or experience is to learn. Decide to act on the intent.
- **Suspend expectations.** When you want to learn some-

thing, it is easy to slip away from intending to learn to an expectation of how fast you'll learn or how easy it will be. Lifelong learners allow the learning to unfold over time, not according to a predetermined schedule.

- **Look the fool.** A true learner is willing to be clumsy or awkward at first. Try to understand the paradox, 'If it's worth doing well, it's worth doing poorly'. In other words, you will make mistakes in the beginning (you'll do poorly) at what you intend to master (what's worth doing well). Learning can be untidy and you may look foolish as you learn, but the lifelong learner values each step along the way.
- **Ask questions.** When you're a lifelong learner, you are willing to expose the fact that you don't know. Your openness to learning is expressed by your willingness to ask questions, even at the risk that others will think the question is 'dumb'. The lifelong learner recognises, as did Socrates, that questions stimulate learning. Challenge yourself to ask ten questions about everything you want to learn.
- **Be humble.** This principle is captured well in the phrase, 'The more I learn, the less I know'. Accept your not knowing as normal. The lifelong learner doesn't expect to know all there is to know about everything. *Not* to know is the more common state of affairs – especially when you consider that over 50,000 new books are released each year, and the amount of available information doubles every three years.
- **Seek the truth.** At heart, lifelong learners want to know the truth. In pursuit of that truth, they stay open to all learning. Truth is understood as something we can only approximate with our current knowledge and experience. To reach truth is a lifetime task.
- **Be ready and patient.** Be kind to yourself as you learn. Sometimes the timing is just not right. 'To everything there is a season', and learning is no exception. Practise recognising the difference between your resistance and readiness. A tulip doesn't resist blooming in the winter, it is simply waiting for its time in the spring. Be sensitive to the

building blocks that need to be in place before you can learn a skill or something about yourself.

Checklist
Identify blocks to openness
Just as there are qualities that enable you to open the door to learning, there are qualities that shut that door. Read through this list and tick the blocks to openness that you realise are impairing your learning process.

☐ I want to look good to protect my self-esteem.
☐ I tend to be a 'know-all'.
☐ I can never work things out on my own.
☐ That method just won't work.
☐ That teacher/instructor isn't doing a good job/isn't explaining things properly.
☐ I don't trust myself to retain this knowledge.
☐ Others won't respect me if I don't know everything.
☐ I have to be perfect.
☐ I couldn't learn it before, and I can't now either.
☐ My way is best, no matter what.

Risk taking

Inherent in most learning is taking risks. At any learning moment there is the risk of looking the fool, which we have discussed. There is also a risk associated with changing your behaviour. You risk shaking up your current beliefs and values when you learn. You take a chance on making mistakes. You put your current level of competence on the line to try doing something in a new way, in which you aren't yet competent. The list of risks is a long one.

More important than our list of risks, however, is your list. From your own perspective, what do you risk when you put yourself into a learning situation?

_____

_____

How do you feel about taking risks?

Because learning and risk taking are so closely associated, it's important to take time to reflect on your own personal risk-taking behaviour. Life is certainly not linear, but for now, imagine your life to be like the line below. At the left end of the life-line is birth, and at the right end is death.

A sample life-line has been completed to get you started. Above the life-line, write the risks that you have taken in your life. This part of the exercise is relatively easy for most people. The more difficult part is writing down the risks that you *didn't* take, below the life-line. You will need a period of quiet reflection to get in touch with the risks you haven't taken. To get the maximum learning from this exercise, give yourself 30 minutes to complete both parts.

Sample

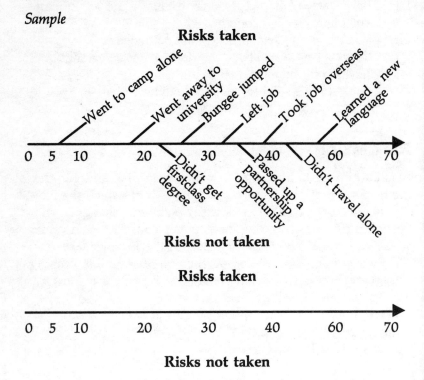

After completing your personal risk life-line, answer these questions:

1. What have you learned about yourself through the risks you've taken?

   _____

   _____

2. When do you tend to take risks?

   _____

   _____

3. At moments of choice, do you tend to move towards, learning (growth), or to maintain the status quo?

   _____

   _____

4. What have been the outcomes of the risks you've taken?

   _____

   _____

5. What have been the outcomes of the risks you haven't taken?

   _____

   _____

6. What relationship do you observe between your willingness to take risks and your perception of yourself as a reluctant, leisurely or lifelong learner?

   _____

   _____

Your personal responsibility for learning

No one can make you learn. No one but you is responsible for your learning. If you happen to feel bored in your current job, that is not someone else's fault. The boredom is *your personal responsibility*. There are things you can do, already outlined in this book, to ease the boredom. It is not the responsibility of your organisation or your bosses to make your work stimulating and meaningful.

Learning means applying what you know, and changing your behaviour based on what you discover. No one can do this for you. Anyone can tell you the secrets of good health, or success, or how to be happy, but only you can apply that knowledge to your life. In the application is the learning.

So if you've been blaming others, the time to stop is *now*. It's time to grow up and take responsibility for yourself, your life and what you're getting out of it. If you don't like the results you're getting, try something new. And if you don't like the way information is presented to you, take responsibility for telling people how you learn best. (You'll find more about his subject in the later section, 'The seven intelligences'.)

For the person who takes responsibility for his own learning, regardless of what support the organisation may provide, there are two benefits: First, he receives the joy and pleasure that are intrinsic to learning. Second, what he's learned can never be taken away. If your organisation doesn't acknowledge or reward learning, be ready to find one that does!

Leslie Charles, President of US company Trainingworks, suggests any person can use a *learning log* to support his or her own learning. Each day, choose one behaviour you want to practise, and write it down in a notebook. At the end of the day, make notes on your progress. This simple learning log will help you to make learning a conscious choice each day. Here are some examples of learning goals: maintain a positive attitude; pay attention to how I use my body at the computer; smile more.

In addition to using a learning log for your own learning, you can share it with people in your organisation. What would you like to focus on learning today? To help yourself get started, complete the following sentences:

I want to learn more about _____

I want to practise _____

I want to research _____

Corporate trainers, chairmen, managing directors and others directly concerned about transforming an organisation into a learning organisation need to remember that each person in the company will make a personal choice about his learning. Not everyone will be a lifelong learner. Leisurely learners have the potential to become lifelong learners if they see that learning is rewarded. Reluctant learners can be helped to find a place outside the organisation, where perhaps they will become leisurely or lifelong learners.

Discovery vs Judgement

Dana Gribben, a speech coach in San Francisco, teaches a very important lesson about judgement:

'When you judge, you aren't participating any more.'

Think about that for a moment. Judgement prevents learning. When you judge, you're engaged in a closed-loop interaction with yourself. For example, have you ever attended a training programme and along the way thought to yourself, 'What a silly exercise', or perhaps, 'This is so basic, I bet I've done this exercise a dozen times! At that moment you are not doing the exercise. You are not participating and you are not learning. You've removed yourself from what is really happening. As long as you're judging, you can't be learning.

So what can you do to counteract the tendency to judgement that comes quickly and easily to most of us? Most of us judge so often that we aren't even aware of it. We may judge ourselves, others or a situation. The first step is to catch yourself in the middle of judgement. Then, trade in your judgement for *discovery*.

Discovery is an attitude that keeps you open to learning. Don't try to decide if you like or dislike, agree or disagree. Simply look to see what is. Explore it. The discoveries you make may be about yourself, the situation or the specific content or skill that you're learning. With this attitude, there is something to be learned in any situation.

Creative or reactive–responsive?

Robert Fritz, in his book *The Path of Least Resistance*, laid out two alternative ways to live.* He calls one orientation *the creative*, and the other orientation *reactive–responsive*.

Most people live from the orientation of the reactive–responsive. In that orientation, you react to what life gives you. You respond to the situations in which you find yourself. Consequently, you often feel powerless to control your life or its events. 'Some people have all the luck', you think. Their lives apparently flow, while you're stuck with bad luck and lousy breaks. If this is your orientation to life, most of your learning is probably accidental and retrospective.

In sharp contrast, from the orientation of the creative, you are empowered to decide what *you* want out of life. Using the tools Fritz outlines in his book, you can go about the process of creating the outcomes you want, proactively deciding what you want to learn in your life and not leaving it to chance. Lifelong learners live from the orientation of the creative.

Working through creative tension

At the core of creative orientation is the task of managing the *creative tension* between your current reality and your vision of what you want. As shown in the following graphic, you start with a vision, something you want to create in your life. Think now about something you want to learn. Describe it as clearly and vividly as you can, so that you know you'll recognise it

---

* Robert Fritz, *The Path of Least Resistance*. Salem, Mass: DMA Inc, 1984.

when you get it. Then tell yourself the truth about your current reality. What is your situation now? Include in your description of current reality any feelings you have about where you are in relation to your goal. The gap between your vision and current reality is called creative tension.

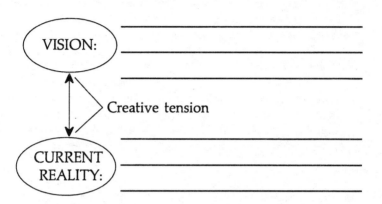

There are two ways to resolve creative tension. One is to drop the vision. In this way the tension is eliminated. Of course, if this is your way of resolving the tension, your self-respect and esteem will also suffer a blow. The second way is to bring your current reality into alignment with your vision. That technique is the way of the orientation of the creative. It's also the way of the lifelong learner.

Case study
Using creative tension

Here's an example of using creative orientation in real life. The author travels a good deal, and decided she wanted to feel safe when out alone. She also wanted to become physically fit. That was her vision. Learning the martial art *aikido* seemed an excellent way to achieve both these goals. Her current reality was that she had no experience with a martial art and was afraid of being thrown. Nor had she ever participated in a regular exercise programme. The gap between where she was

> (unskilled and untoned) and where she wanted to be (strong and competent) was the creative tension.
>
> During years of practice there were many times when getting to class was difficult; when she didn't want to do what was necessary to reach the vision. As motivation, she asked herself a simple question: 'Do I still want the vision?' The answer was yes. However, she still wanted to stay at home sometimes, spend time with the family or read a good book. Those feelings became part of her current reality. There were many times when she drove to the *dojo* (the place of practice) thinking, 'I don't want to go.'
>
> Dropping the goal would be the easier path. But she still wants the goal, and holds the same vision. Until she achieves that vision, a gap will exist between the current reality and the goal. In the meantime, however, she'll be able to see how current reality has advanced towards the vision.

As you work to transform your company into a learning organisation, remember that the gap between where you are and where you want to be is the very fuel that will enable you to reach your vision. The orientation of the creative allows you to concentrate less on problems, and more on challenges.

Harnessing the natural desire to learn

It's a well-known motivation principle that people do things for their own reasons, not for someone else's. This principle applies just as clearly to learning. The more you understand what is behind someone's desire to learn, the more you can support them in their learning. In the process, you'll enhance the learning that's occurring overall in your organisation. Let's examine some motivations to learn.

- **Curiosity.** We've talked about this as a natural drive towards learning that exists in human beings at birth. That innate curiosity has been encouraged to a degree in all of us. Some people in your organisation will want to learn about everything, and their motive is pure and simple: curiosity.
- **Self-protection.** In our rapidly changing environment, many people realise that to keep their job, they must

continuously develop new skills. Consequently, some people will take courses, seek out mentors, and maximise other learning opportunities, not because they see intrinsic value in learning but because they want to insulate themselves against change. This type of learning is motivated by fear.

- **To fulfil a purpose.** Some people come to work for something to do, but many are there because they want to do something. They'd like to touch lives and make a difference. For them, work is a passion or a calling. Listening to this inner call, they are motivated to learn whatever will bring them into closer alignment with their purpose as they see it.

- **Reward or profit.** Certainly there are people who are motivated by financial gain. And in some fields, the more you learn, the more you earn. In professions such as social work, psychology and accounting, a person who achieves certification or licensing will command a higher salary. Some companies base their pay scale in part upon the number of courses taken and successfully completed, or may grant jobs and promotions when certain courses or educational requirements are met. Thus, some people are motivated to learn because of tangible reward.

- **Through painful or negative experiences.** Anyone who has been in the workforce for a number of years has probably at some time worked with a difficult or ineffective boss. This apparently negative experience can actually be a profound learning situation. By observing the behaviour of the difficult person, you learn how *not* to behave. You discover that the way you are being managed is different from the way you want to be managed. This is an outstanding example of the advantage given by an attitude of discovery; being non-judgemental can turn a painful experience into insight and growth.

- **Fun.** Learning can indeed be fun. Everyone needs a little play in their lives, and learning can be a way to have that. Increasingly, games are a part of learning programmes, and laughter comes out of board rooms and classrooms everywhere. The most effective foreign-language programme in the world, according to *The Learning Revolution* by Dryden and Vos,* is from Accelerated Learning Systems of Aston Clinton in Buckinghamshire. It combines music, stories, and play acting into a highly successful programme that is fun and effective. Children learn through play, so why not adults?

- **When expectations aren't met.** Suppose you're chairing a meeting and you don't get through the agenda in the time allowed. You may feel discomfort because *your expectations haven't been met*. This is a powerful motivator for learning. When expectations aren't met, there's an opportunity to set the orientation of the creative in motion. If you want your next meeting to run more smoothly, you'll want to learn how to plan an agenda. You have a goal, current reality doesn't match the goal, and so you'll make an effort to bring the two into alignment through learning.

- **For future focus.** People who work in a rapidly developing field or industry and want to stay in that industry another five years or so must invest learning time *now* if they want to be a real part of that future. For example, in professional speaking and training, multimedia presentations will be the standard visual aid of the future. The motivation to learn about graphics, LCD panels and other projection devices is thus directly inspired by a desire to remain in the field in the future.

- **It's compulsory.** Making training compulsory is another way to motivate through fear. Whenever a particular training session or skill is made *mandatory*, people look for the consequence if they don't learn. Depending upon the perceived severity of the consequence, obligation may or may not motivate. This strategy reflects the control imposed by hierarchical organisations of the past, and will be of decreasing use in the new learning organisation. Because certain programmes are required by law, this motivator may never disappear completely, however.

---

* Gordon Dryden and Jeanette Vos, *The Learning Revolution*. Rolling Hills Estates, California: Jalmar Press, 1994.

- **Enjoyment.** Some people simply love learning! Learning is a pleasure in and of itself. It leads to self-esteem and confidence. It energises and stimulates the person − a true natural high.

In addition to these ten motivators for learning, there may be others that you would like to include. It's important for each learner, yourself included, to know why and when he or she is most likely to learn. Now that we've examined the why, let's take a look at the when. To uncover this for yourself, begin by describing three significant learning experiences in your life. These may be job related or personal.

Learning experience 1: _____

_____

Learning experience 2: _____

_____

Learning experience 3: _____

_____

Reflect on these three learning experiences and ask yourself what motivated you to learn. Was it the same motivator in each situation? Were there several reasons you learned in that situation? Did something motivate you that wasn't on the list you just studied?

The seven intelligences

Howard Gardner, in his book *Frames of Mind*, identifies seven different *intelligences*.* Most people are only aware of the ones that are typically emphasised in school, such as maths and English. Discovering all the other intelligences changes an

* Howard Gardner, *Frames of Mind*. London, Fontana Press, 1993.

individual's self-perception, and opens them to learning what they may have previously avoided.

Lifelong learners know their strengths and make the most of them. As you read through the seven intelligences, tick the ones that you think are strongest for you. What is the relationship between your intelligences and what you prefer to learn? Is there a relationship between what you resist learning and your weakest intelligences?

☐ **1. Musical.** This intelligence emerges before any other and is not highly valued in some cultures. If musical aptitude is one of your preferred intelligences, you're aware that you carry sounds in your head. Composers have this intelligence, and it primarily uses the auditory channel.

☐ **2. Linguistic.** Unlike musical intelligence, linguistic intelligence emerges more slowly and often does not peak until age 50, 60 or even 70. That's why many writers do their best work in their later years. Poets, writers and people who love the sound of words and their shades of meaning have this intelligence. Reading, writing and communicating with words comes from this intelligence. Linguistic intelligence is highly valued at school. Like music, it uses the auditory channel as well.

☐ **3. Logical/Mathematical.** Scientists, lawyers and mathematicians have this intelligence. It begins with objects to be counted and becomes quite abstract. In fact, the reasoning of someone with logical/mathematical intelligence can become so complex that the average person has trouble understanding. Chess players have this intelligence. It peaks early, usually by age 30 to 40, and also arrives early, as does musical intelligence. Logical/Mathematical intelligence is the other aptitude highly valued in school.

☐ **4. Spatial.** Like logical/mathematical intelligence, spatial intelligence is involved with objects – recognising them in different elements or when they've been transformed.

This is the intelligence of the graphic artist, architect, navigator and pilot. It does not deteriorate with age and is 'right brain' oriented.

☐ **5. Body/Kinaesthetic.** People with this intelligence use their bodies in a controlled way. Dancers, mimes, martial artists and athletes have body/kinaesthetic intelligence. They can handle objects skilfully and develop mechanical skills.

☐ **6. Intrapersonal.** This intelligence varies by culture, but the focus is on the inner life, feelings and intuitions. Spiritual teachers and religious leaders have this intrapersonal intelligence. Introspection is part of this intelligence, as well.

☐ **7. Interpersonal.** This intelligence, too, is influenced by your culture. It has an outward focus, involving relation-ships, detecting the feelings of others, and knowing oneself in relation to others. Salespeople and motivators have this intelligence.

Tell yourself the truth about current reality

An important part of the orientation of the creative is to tell yourself the truth about current reality. If your vision is to become a lifelong learner or to help someone else become one, you need to describe honestly and accurately where you are now. Though you may start out awkward, uncertain or scared, there is no need to judge your current reality. It is what it is. The more you know about it, the better you can plan to close the gap between it and your vision.

As an aspiring lifelong learner, describe in a paragraph your current reality.

_____

_____

_____

_____

Use the same process to describe your organisation. Assuming the vision is to create a learning organisation, what is the current reality of your company?

_____

_____

_____

_____

_____

What follows below is a list of some typical components of current reality. Do any of these sound like yours or your organisation's?

I'm too busy

If you have a report due on Friday, how can you possibly be expected to commit a day to a training programme? If you have a budget to prepare, why do you have to spend time reflecting on the effectiveness of a staff meeting? When there's a deadline to meet, how do you make time to practise a new communication model with a co-worker?

These are real concerns and challenges for someone becoming a lifelong learner and for a group becoming a learning organisation. The critical issue is, what do you value? To what do you aspire? If learning is integrated into who you are and the way you work, it is no longer something that's outside your mainstream job activities. Learning *is* your job. Time invested in learning today saves time tomorrow.

Fear

By definition, when you're learning, you're on your growing edge. Depending upon the type of learning you're engaged in, you will experience more or less fear associated with it. For example, if you're in incremental learning (how to use a new feature of a computer program you already use, for instance), there will be less fear than if you're making a paradigm shift to a new procedure for getting the work done.

Looking more deeply into the issue, what is it that you fear? Often you are afraid that you won't 'get in'. The learning will be too difficult, and you'll look stupid. You'll be left behind your peers. These are issues of self-esteem.

You may also fear that the learning won't be applied. Why invest the time, especially when you're so busy, just to find out it was wasted time because the new method won't be implemented? Or perhaps the fear is that you'll discover something about yourself that you don't really want to know. Or you might need to change your patterns with new learning.

The most effective response to fear is to acknowledge it, name it, and move forward towards your vision. Don't make the mistake of letting fear give you the message, 'Don't do it'.

What other reasons can you think of for a person being afraid to learn?

Weak follow-through
It's critical to remember that learning is not the same thing as knowing. Learning takes place when behaviour changes. You may 'know' that exercise is good for you, but until you 'do' an exercise programme, true learning, hasn't taken place. You can 'know' that communication is enhanced when you practise reflective listening, but the learning of that habit takes place in the day-to-day, unconsciously competent application of what you know.

Too often we gain knowledge and feel convinced about the benefits of applying the knowledge to our lives. Then, when it comes to the follow-through of implementing what we know, we get sloppy. With weak follow-through, the result is less learning than is otherwise possible.

What is the secret, then, to applying learning? There is no

secret. You need to decide to apply what you know. Until you make learning a priority, it will happen only by accident.

Lack of vision
In a learning project for a department of local government, the training facilitator met each top manager for an individual consultation about his or her learning goals for the coming year. One manager, in her job for 15 years, said, 'There's nothing I want to learn. I like my job and I have only 17 years until I retire.' This person had no vision for herself. She was content at the moment and could see no value in learning. In further discussions, she went on to say she knew her job very well and there was nothing new to learn.

Unfortunately, some people drift into learning arrogance, living from the orientation of reactive–responsive. When they realise their skills haven't kept up with the new ways of doing things, it may be too late to catch up. No matter what your current station in life, there is always something to be learned. Take control of your life and decide what you want to learn.

Lack of personal resources
It's not uncommon to want to pursue an academic degree and be blocked by inadequate financial resources or substantial family commitments. Or perhaps you are put off by the discovery that you don't have a 'natural gift' for a skill that you want to learn.

Most of these barriers can be overcome; however, it may not happen on your personal time schedule. The degree may need to wait until your children are older. An acting career may have to become an avocation rather than a vocation. Use your creativity and the mentors in your life to strategise ways of responding to insufficient personal resources.

Low self-esteem
Self-esteem is how you feel about yourself. When you like yourself, you're more apt to have self-confidence and to trust yourself. Without self-esteem it's hard to believe in yourself. Without self-confidence you may be more hesitant about

learning opportunities, to doubt your ability to accomplish something. This negative self-talk will kill your desire to learn.

If you experience feelings of low self-esteem, self-doubt or worthlessness, your first learning assignment is to build up your esteem. One critical tool is building success experiences of 'I can ...' Get started today!

Judgement
When you're not 'getting it', when you feel uncomfortable, when you can't see the purpose of something – that's when it's easy to quiet your discomfort with a negative judgement.

Whether your judgement is directed at yourself or outside yourself, that judgement shuts down your ability to learn and damages your self-esteem. Try to catch yourself as you're in the midst of a judgement. Then simply name what you are doing. 'Oh, I'm judging.' Do not criticise yourself for judging, either. Saying something like, 'There I go again, judging. I make no progress. What's wrong with me anyway?' doesn't solve anything. Stick to a simple naming of what you are doing. Then refocus your attention on the learning task at hand. This skill in handling judgement as you learn can be applied to all areas of your life, with dramatic results. You'll increase self-esteem, develop inner calm, and reduce stress. Try it.

Five strategies to manage creative tension

You have a vision of yourself becoming a lifelong learner, and you've told yourself the truth about current reality. How will you close the gap between the two? Jot down your ideas on the diagram below. Then check your ideas against those presented in this section.

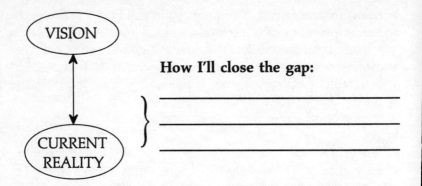

Here's an acronym to help you remember the key strategies for managing creative tension, which is the gap between your vision and current reality. Take PRIDE with you whenever you want to learn!

P .... People
R .... Research, read
I .... Introspection
D .... Do
E .... obsErve

Here are examples of each of these tools to get you started.

People

- Ask questions
- Seek out a mentor
- Listen to what people say in meetings
- Network
- Join and participate in professional associations
- Pick up the phone and call someone
- Talk to people.

Research, read

- Subscribe to relevant journals
- Go to the library
- Read regularly
- Subscribe to an online information service, such as CompuServe

- Learn to navigate the Internet
- Make friends with your local librarian
- Attend conferences, institutes, training sessions
- Seek exposure to cutting-edge ideas
- Frequent bookstores
- Read book reviews
- Subscribe to audio learning programmes.

Introspection

- Take time to reflect
- Think through an action before you take it
- Study the way you handled yourself in a particular situation
- Analyse
- Look deeply into situations
- Question with the intent to understand rather than judge
- Keep a journal
- Write out your ideas as a concept or white paper.

Do

- Try it
- Experiment
- Use trial and error
- Implement
- Throw yourself into the middle of the thing
- Get your hands dirty
- Take action – move your body, hands, feet
- Feel it in your body
- Take action
- Put your pen to paper and start writing
- Put your fingers on the keyboard and start typing
- Pick up the phone and dial
- Just do it.

ObsErve

- Watch others
- Look for role models
- Pay attention
- Don't judge

- Seek to understand what you see
- Study facial expressions
- Examine others' behaviour
- Study how others handle situations
- Use all your senses.

Remember that others are observing you as they learn. Are you modelling the behaviour of a lifelong learner?

The power in your learning comes when you can integrate all five of these PRIDE strategies. Remember them by letting each one be represented by a finger on one hand. The easiest way to open a door is to push it with all five fingers. Let PRIDE open your doors to learning.

Summary

In a changing world, learning is one of the few competitive advantages. If *Creating a Learning Organisation* has fulfilled its purpose, you now have the guidance you need to turn your organisation into a learning organisation.